Georg Forster

Sketches of the Mythology and Customs of the Hindoos

Georg Forster

Sketches of the Mythology and Customs of the Hindoos

ISBN/EAN: 9783337012557

Printed in Europe, USA, Canada, Australia, Japan

Cover: Foto ©ninafisch / pixelio.de

More available books at **www.hansebooks.com**

SKETCHES

OF THE

MYTHOLOGY

AND

CUSTOMS

OF THE

HINDOOS.

LONDON:
PRINTED IN THE YEAR
MDCCLXXXV.

SKETCHES

OF THE

MYTHOLOGY

AND

CUSTOMS

OF THE

HINDOOS,

MOST RESPECTFULLY INSCRIBED

TO THE HONORABLE THE

COURT OF DIRECTORS

OF THE

EAST-INDIA COMPANY,

BY THEIR DUTIFUL SERVANT,

GEORGE FORSTER.

London,
July, 1785.

*T*HE following cursory dissertation, which has been extracted from private letters, the Author is induced to lay before the Public, from a desire of throwing some light on a subject, hitherto, but partially known in Europe; and also, with the view of prompting others, whose bent of disposition and conveniency of situation may lead them into such researches, to enlarge on so curious a matter.

To hold out an asylum to the memory of an antient, and a once great people, who before the fall

of

of their empire were amply enlightened by science, and who were governed by a system of laws and policy, which had the most salutary effects in rendering them virtuous and happy, will yield a sufficient compensation to the man of philanthropy, for every difficulty that he may encounter in the pursuit of a study which will be found, it is to be feared, entangled in some discouraging perplexities.

Extract of a Letter, dated at Banaris in September, 1782.

THE city of Banaris, in point of its wealth, coftly buildings, and the number of its inhabitants, is claffed in the firft rank of thofe now remaining in Hinduftan, in the poffeffion of the Hindoos.

To defcribe, with any degree of precifion, the various temples dedicated in this place to the almoft innumerable

numerable deities, and to explain the origin of their foundation, with the neceſſary arrangement, would require a knowledge, infinitely ſuperior to mine, in the myſterious rites of the Hindoo mythology.

They are, at this day, enveloped in ſuch impenetrable obſcurity, that even thoſe Pundits who are the moſt ſkilfully verſed in the Sumſcrit,* are not able to throw on them lights ſufficiently clear for the rendering them comprehenſible to the generality of the people.

But as ſome relation, though imperfect, of a city ſo famous in Hinduſtan, and now ſo well known in

* The language in which all their ſacred legends are preſerved.

Europe

Europe for having been one of the grand fources of the religious worfhip of the Hindoos, and being the chief repofitory of what fcience yet exifts among them, may not be unacceptable to you, together with fome curfory inveftigations of the mythology of Brimha, the tafk fhall be attempted with every attention to the fubject, and with the ftricteft adherence to truth.

If errors fhould arife on the treating on a matter hitherto flightly difcuffed, and from its complication exceedingly abftrufe, I have to intreat your liberal indulgence; and that though miftaken in my conclufions, you will give me fome commendation were it only for the endeavour of adminiftering to a rational pleafure.

At the distance of eight miles from the city of Banaris, as it is approached on the river from the eastward, the eye is attracted by the view of two lofty minarets, which were erected by the order of Aurungzebe, on the foundation of an ancient Hindoo temple, dedicated to the Mhah Deve, or the God Eishwer.

The raising, on such sacred ruins, this towering Mahometan pile, which from its elevated height seems to look down with triumph and exaltation on the fallen state of a city so profoundly revered by the Hindoos, would appear to have been prompted to the mind of Aurungzebe by a bigotted and intemperate desire of insulting their religion.

If

If such was his wish, it hath been most completely fulfilled.

For the Hindoos consider this monument as a disgraceful record of a foreign yoke, and as proclaiming to every stranger, that their favorite city has been debased, and the worship of their gods defiled.

From the top of the minarets there is seen an entire and a very beautiful prospect of Banaris, which occupies a space of about two miles and a half along the northern bank of the Ganges, and a mile inland from the river.

Many of the houses are remarkably high, some of them having six and seven stories, and built of a stone resembling that sort found in the quar-
ries

ries of Portland, and which abounds in this part of the country.

The streets, wherein these lofty buildings are situated, are so narrow, as not to admit of two carriages a-breast.

The consequence of this large city being constructed on so confined a plan, is, that the air, from being deprived of a free circulation, becomes putrid and obnoxious, and in particular seasons causes fevers of a malignant species, and severe bilious obstructions.

In addition to this pernicious effect, proceeding from a corrupted atmosphere, there is at most times an intolerable stench, which arises from the many tanks dispersed in the different

ferent quarters of the town, whofe waters and borders are appropriated to the common ufe of the inhabitants.

The filth alfo, which is indifcriminately thrown into the ftreets, and there left expofed, (for the Hindoos poffefs but a fmall portion of a general cleanlinefs) add to the compound of ill fmells which fo much offend the noftrils of every one entering this city.

The irregular and very confined mode which has been invariably adhered to in the conftruction of Banaris, has, in a great meafure, deftroyed the pleafing effects which fymmetry and arrangement would otherwife have beftowed on a city, entitled from its numerous and expenfive habitations,

to

to demand a preference to any capital which I have seen in India.

In the researches which I have been enabled to make into the principles of the Hindoo religion, I have received great aid from a converfant knowledge of the Mhahrattah language, and an acquaintance, though trivial, with the Sumfcrit.

The ufe of this laft tongue is now chiefly confined to a particular fect of Bramins, who officiate in the character of priefts, and it hath ever been adopted as the channel of conveying to the Hindoos, the effentials of their religion, with all the various forms of their worfhip.

The Sumfcrit is a fonorous language, its periods flow with great
boldnefs,

boldnefs, and terminate in a cadence peculiarly mufical, and it abounds in a pith and concifenefs far fuperior to any other, with which I am in any wife acquainted.

An extract of a floke or ftanza, which has been quoted by Mr. Halhed, is a ftriking teftimony of the nervous compofition, and the laconic turn of the Sumfcrit.

As it is a ftanza of only four lines, I will infert it, and alfo attempt the tranflation.

Pĭtāche rĕnĕwān fhĕtrōō
Father — in debt — enemy
Mātāh fhĕtrōō   rĕfhĕlēnēē
Mother — enemy — extravagant or immoral
Bhārĭăh rŭpĕwūttēē fhĕtrōō
Wife — beautiful — enemy
Pōōtrĕ fhĕtrōō n'pūndĭtāh
Son — enemy — unlearned

The mother who hath loſt her fame,
The fire profuſe, and foe to ſhame,
    Are to their race a peſt.
A bride's ſoft joys oft' thorns implant,
And he, who roams in folly's haunt,
    Deſtroys his father's reſt.

The Hindoos believe in one God, without beginning and without end; on whom they beſtow, deſcriptive of his power, a variety of epithets.

But the moſt common appellation, and which conveys the ſublimeſt ſenſe of his greatneſs, is, Sree Mun Narrain, the univerſal Protector.

The Hindoos, in their firſt and grand ſupplication to the Deity, addreſs him as endowed with the three

attri-

attributes, of omnipotence, omnipreſence and omniſcience; which, in the Sumſcrit, are expreſſed by the terms, neer anjin, neer akar, and neer goon.

Though this explanation may not, in literary ſtrictneſs, compriſe in it the preciſe meaning of the Engliſh text, it doth ſo virtually, and in the ampleſt ſenſe.

A circumſtance which forcibly ſtruck my attention, was the Hindoo belief of a Trinity.

The perſons are, Sree Mun Narrain, the Mhah Letchimy (a beautiful woman), and a Serpent, which are emblematical of ſtrength, love and wiſdom.

These persons, by the Hindoos, are supposed to be wholly indivisible.

The one is three, and the three are one.

In the beginning they say, that the Deity created three men, to whom he gave the names of Brimha, Vyftnou, and Shevah.*

To the first, was committed the power of creating mankind, to the second of cherishing them, and to the third that of restraining and correcting them.

Brimha, at one breath, formed the human kind out of the four elements; amongst which he infused, as I understood the intrepretation, a vacuum.

* Often called Eishwer, or the Mhah Deve.

Before the creation of man, Sree Mun Narrain framed the world out of a chaos; it was covered with the waters, furrounded by an utter darknefs, and inhabited by a demon, the fuppofed author of evil, whom the Godhead drove into an abyfs under the earth.

The Hindoos, as Mr. Halhed, in his Tranflation of the Code of Hindoo Laws, has fully and clearly fet forth, are arranged in four grand cafts or tribes*; that of the Bramin, the Chittery, the Bhyfe and the Sooder.

* There is, in India, an aboriginal race of people who are not claffed in any of the fects, and are employed in the meaneft and moft menial offices. They are not permitted to enter any temple of the Hindoos, and in their diet they have no reftriction. On fome parts of the coaft of Choromandel they are called Pariahs, and, in Bengal, Hurrees.

Each

Each of these casts are sub-divided into numerous sects, the particular usages of which are preserved with great care and attentive distinctions.

There is an immense number of sectaries of the same tribe, who do not admit of the intercourse of marriage with each other, or of eating at the same board.

From the best information which I have been enabled to procure, it would seem that the genuine Chittery, or Rajah race, has for a great length of time been extinct, and in its place a spurious tribe has been introduced.

The Hindoos, composing these casts and classes, are ultimately branched out in two divisions; the one denominated

minated the Vyſtnou Bukht, and the other the Shevah Bukht.

The followers of the firſt are diſtinguiſhed by marking the forehead with a longitudinal, and thoſe of the ſecond with a parallel line.

In the temple of Vyſtnou, he is worſhipped under the repreſentation of a human figure, having a circle of heads and four hands, emblems of an all-ſeeing, and an all-provident Being.

The repreſentation of a fabulous bird, on which he is ſuppoſed to ride, and denotive of the velocity of his motion, is frequently placed in front of his image.

Shevah or Eiſhwer, or as he is uſually called by the Hindoos, the Mhah

Mhah Deve, or great God, is reprefented by a compound figure, defcribing the male and female parts of generation, and defigned as fymbols of procreation and fecundity.

Thefe faculties or qualities being held amongft the Hindoos as the choiceft bleffings, and the deprivation of them deemed a fevere reproach and misfortune.

Facing this defignation of the Mhah Deve, is generally feen, in a fuppliant pofture, the image of a cow, which is faid to have derived its peculiarly facred qualities from having been chofen by this god as his favorite conveyance.

The more enlightened Pundits tell you, that this animal hath been preferved from flaughter from its great utility

utility to man; it being his ableſt aſſiſtant in the labors of the field, and the chief ſupport in his immediate maintenance.

Not to ſay that it argues a ſound policy to ſtamp this creature with ſo ſacred a mark; for were its fleſh eaten, as Hinduſtan is productive of but few horſes, the various branches of agriculture would ſuffer an eſſential injury.

Another figure repreſents Shev'ah with four hands (holding in them different emblems of his power) and five heads; four of which are directed to the cardinal points, and the fifth is placed with the face upwards, in the act of contemplating the grand Deity.

D After

After the service which Brimhah has performed on earth, it would reasonably be concluded, that his praise for the obligations which mankind have received at his hands, in some degree, would be conformable to his works.

But the Hindoos have not dedicated one temple to his honor, nor have they set apart or sanctified one day in remembrance of his deeds.

It would redound but little to my credit, were I to insert in this place, the reason alledged in their religious tracts, for this seeming neglect of Brimhah.

It is a tale framed to amuse the credulous Hindoo, and procure a meal to an artful priest.

This

This oftenſible want of attention to the memory of Brimhah, may on a more abſtracted ground be attributed to the opinion, that the powers of procreation having been once ſet in action, and operating by a law, general and undeviating, whoſe immediate benefits exiſts and are evidently diſplayed in its effects, there was no neceſſity of commemorating the firſt individual cauſe.

The Hindoos believe implicitly in predeſtination, and in the tranſmigration of the ſoul.

The firſt, as it frequently cramps the genius and obſtructs its progreſſion, yet has a tendency in conſoling them in every misfortune, and adminiſtering to them a comfort in all the untoward events of life.

They say it is the hand of God, which for some inscrutinable purpose directs and impels the actions of his creature.

The doctrine of the metempsychosis restrains them from the use of animal food*; an aliment not necessary, and often attended with pernicious consequences in a hot climate.

This belief has also a strong tendency to infuse into their minds an abhorrence of all sanguinary acts, and to inculcate the virtues of humanity and a general affection.

* This tenet is not at this day strictly adhered to, for the Hindoos of the second and fourth cast occasionally use flesh meats, and the Bramins of Bengal invariably eat fish.

The

The Hindoos compute their grand evolutions of time by Joques, of which they have four, correſponding in their nature with the golden, ſilver, brazen, and iron ages of the antients.

The preſent, they ſay, is the Khullee, or the fourth Joque; and that at the expiration of every age, the Supreme Being has deſtroyed this globe of earth, which has been re-created at the commencement of the one ſucceeding, and that a continued ſucceſſion of Joques will revolve *ad infinitum.*

The records of this ancient and extraordinary people, unfortunately for the learned of the preſent day, teem ſo profuſely with fable, and abound throughout in ſuch extravagant relations

tions of the actions of their demi-gods, greatly similar in their feats to the Bacchus, Hercules, and Theseus of the Greeks, that no rational or satisfactory conclusion can be drawn for any adjustment of chronology.

A Pundit will introduce into his legend a laack* of years with as much facility, and perhaps conviction to himself, as a modern commentator would reduce to his standard half a century.

The principles of the Hindoo religion, with its most essential tenets, were composed, it is asserted, by Brimhah, and comprized in four books, entitled the Baids or Vaids, a word

---

* An hundred thousand.

signifying

signifying mystery in the Sumscrit language.

In that part of the peninsula of India bordering on the Choromandel side, these sacred writings are named the Vaidums.

The Telingahs and the Malabars commonly change the letter B into a V, and invariably terminate all Sumscrit words with an M.

The Shastre, meaning science, is a most voluminous commentary on the Baids; and has been written by various Pundits, for the purpose of illustrating their mythology. From the Shastre proceed those preposterous and irreconcileably superstitious ceremonies which have been dragged by their
doctors

doctors into the Hindoo fyftem of worfhip; all of them tending to fhackle the vulgar mind, and produce in it a flavifh reverence for the tribe of Bramins.

The privilege of reading the Baids and expounding its texts is only allowed to them, and prohibited under fevere penalties from the infpection of the other cafts.

By the fole inveftment of this fingular authority, the prieft is left at liberty to explain the original doctrine as may be the moft conducive in confolidating the power and promoting the interefts of his order.

In the tranfmigration of the foul into different bodies, confifts the various

ous gradations of reward and punishment amongst the Hindoos.

Conformably to their good or evil actions they are transposed into the bodies of such creatures, whether of the human or brute species, as by their conduct, whilst in the occupation of their former tenements, they may have merited.

They do not admit of the infliction of eternal punishment, and shudder at the idea of a belief so disconsonant to the opinion which they have formed of the Supreme Being.

Evil dispositions, they say, are chastised by a confinement in the bodies of those animals whose natures they most resemble, and are constrained to occupy them until their vices are either eradicated,

eradicated, or so purged as that they shall be judged worthy of possessing superior forms.

The good actions of man, the Hindoo law-giver has written, will be rewarded by their being made to personify such beings as enjoy the utmost human happiness.

As that which the magistrate experiences on the just and merciful execution of the trust which has been committed to him; or, that high sense of pleasure which the **man of humanity** partakes of, when he has alleviated the distresses of the unfortunate, or otherwise promoted the welfare of mankind.

The man who is acceptable in the sight of his God, the Hindoo says, will

will copiously imbibe all those heartfelt satisfactions, which are produced from the well performance of the different duties of life.

After having occupied a series of bodies to the approbation of the Deity and his soul, from a pursuit of virtue, shall be purified from the taints of evil, the Hindoo is then admitted to participation of the radiant and never ceasing glory of his first cause.

The soul's receiving this act of bliss, is described, by comparing it to a ray of light, attracted by the grand powers of the sun, to which it shoots with an immense velocity, and is there absorbed in the blaze of splendor.

Yum Durm Rajah officiates in the same capacity amongst the Hindoos, as Minos did in the infernal regions of the antients.

At the tribunal of Yum Durm, all departed fouls are fuppofed to appear, and their actions are proclaimed aloud by this judge, who paffes an immediate fentence.

Should the difpofition of a man have been fo flagitioufly wicked and depraved, as to be judged unworthy even of an introduction into the body of the vileft animal, fuch corporeal torments are impofed on him as may be thought adequate to the tranfgreffion, and the foul is afterwards placed in fome fuitable ftation on earth.

According to the religious traditions of the Hindoos, Sree Mun Narrain, fince the creation of the world, has at
nine

nine different periods affumed incarnated forms for the purpofe of eradicating fome particular evil, or otherwife chaftifing the fins of mankind.

The Hindoos worfhip a fecondary fpecies of deity, which they wildly reckon at the number of the thirty-three krore*, and who in their different functions are defigned to reprefent the multiplied infinitude of power of the Supreme Deity.

From the croud of images which the Bramin has placed in the temples of the Hindoos, they have been branded with the appellation of idolaters, or adorers of many gods.

Let this mode of offering up fupplications

* A krore is a hundred laacks.

plications or thankfgivings to the Supreme Being be difpaffionately examined, and it may be feen, that a perfonification of the attributes of the Deity, is not unfitly adapted to the general comprehenfion.

For thofe, and they compofe a great portion of the people, who, from a want of the requifite education, are not endowed with the ability of reading the praife of God, can with facility conceive an idea of his greatnefs, by contemplating a figure, fculptured with many heads and with many hands, adorned with every fymbol of human power, and beheld by all claffes of men with the utmoft reverence and awe.

Were the origin of emblematical figures deduced with a pofitive degree

of

of certainty, there would remain little doubt of discovering, that they far preceded the use of letters.

The Spanish records mention, that the intelligence of the first arrival of the Europeans on the coast of Mexico, was described to Motezuma by figures painted on cotton cloth.

In a rude society, it was evidently a more easy operation to convey an idea thro' the medium of a simple figure cut in wood or moulded in clay, than to invent an alphabet, and out of it compose an assemblage of words necessary for the formation of a language.

The immense group of Hindoo gods enjoy immortality, which they are gifted with from drinking a beverage, called

called Amrut, and which feems to bear fome analogy to the nectar of Homer's deities.

In their mythology, there is an elegant defcription of nine goddeffes, refembling in a great degree the mufes of the antients, in the nature of their provinces.

There is alfo, moft picturefquely delineated, the God of Love, who has a variety of epithets, all fignificant of the unbounded fway, which he poffeffes over the hearts of men.

His common names are Kaum and Mudden, and he is reprefented as a pleafing youth, armed with a bow and five arrows, denoting the five fenfes, each of which weapon is baited with different qualities of the poifon, which is infufed by the communication of the paffion of love.

A curious picture was found at Tanjore, when the fort was captured, of Kaum riding on an elephant, whofe form was compofed of the figures of feven young women, which were entwined together in fo ingenious and whimfical a manner, that they exhibited an exact fhape of that bulky animal.

In the Bifs Eifhwer Pagoda at Banaris, there is a defign well executed in ftone of the God of the Sun, fitting in a chariot and driving a horfe with twelve heads, allufive of the twelve figns of the Zodiac.

If the perufal of this rough and abbreviated fketch, fhould lead on any gentleman

gentleman eftablifhed in this part of the country, and poffeffing an inclination to this caft of inveftigation, to profecute a farther and a more minute inquiry into the principles of the Hindoo religion, I fhall deem the trivial labour undergone in this refearch, as moft amply compenfated.

Without putting etymological proofs to the torture, or moulding to the fhape of his fyftem the generally unfatisfactory and deceitful aids of chronology, the careful obferver might be enabled to trace fome points of the religious worfhip of the Hindoo into Egypt.

There he would difcover the facred Bull, or the Cow of Shevah, placed high in the holy legends of the Coptis; he would fee the Snake, one of

the

the mysterious associates of Sree Mun Narrain, devoutly revered by that nation, as an hieroglyphical emblem of wisdom and longevity.

It would also appear, that the Onion so frequently mentioned by historians and travellers, as held in profound veneration amongst the Egyptians, is no less marked with reverence in Hindustan; where, though the use of a vegetable diet, is so strongly inculcated, and with a few deviations, commonly adopted, the Onion is forbidden to some of the sects of priests; and, in the upper part of India, when an oath, on which a matter of consequence depends, is administered, the Bramin frequently introduces the Onion to render the ceremony more awful.

F 2   On

On comparing the religious tenets, and the forms of worſhip of the Hindoos, with thoſe of the ancients, there appears in the functions of ſome of the deities, a ſtrong uniformity of likeneſs, which is not unreaſonably placed in the ſame point of view, and were it poſſible to procure a deſcription of the occupations and the various powers of the Hindoo ſubaltern gods, it might be found that the celeſtial group of the weſtern pantheon, had been ſelected from the divine aſſembly of Brimhah.

The Egyptians and the Greeks in their commerce with India, thro' the channel of the Red Sea, have left, I am induced to believe, many tokens behind them of their connection with the Hindoos.

In the collection of a gentleman at Banaris, there are several valuable antiques, which he purchased of the merchants of that city; one of which, representing a Grecian matron, is cut in a style bearing every mark of a masterly hand.

There is another, on which Cleopatra is exhibited in the act of being bitten by the asp.

The same gentleman had in his possession a Medusa's head, on an emerald, found also at Banaris, which he sent to England, and it has there been acknowledged to be genuinely Greek.

There was procured at Guzerat, some years ago, a very high finished cameo, whereon, Hercules flaying the Nemean Lion, was executed in a most beautiful and striking manner.

These

Thefe circumftances are adverted to with fome fhew of evincing, that during the intercourfe which exifted between the natives of Egypt and of India, the former might have introduced into their country, with the rare and luxurious products of Hinduftan, certain tenets and ceremonies of the Hindoo mythology.

In confidering of the tract by which thefe antiques were brought into India, I muft not omit mentioning, that they might have found their way into that country in the cabinets of fome of the Muffulman conquerors; who, in the more early period of their empire, were as warm and as enthufiaftic admirers of Greek productions and literature as ever the Romans were; and it is a fact, in need of no illuftration,

illuftration, that the revival of letters and the arts, after Rome had been fwallowed up in Gothic ruin, received the moft potent aid from the Arabian Kaliph, Haroun ul Rachid.

I am fincerely to lament that my knowledge in aftronomy is fo very confined, that I am almoft wholly incapacitated from defcribing the attainment which the Bramins had arrived at in that fcience, long, previoufly to the æra in which it flourifhed in the weftern world.

The Zodiac, with its twelve figns, is well known to them; and they have beftowed on the feven days, commencing the week with Sunday, the names of the planets.

The folar year of the Hindoos confifts of twelve months, making three hundred and fixty days, and once in three years they annex an additional month, for the inclufion of thofe days which are wanting to compleat the exact fpace of time required by the earth in making its triennial revolution round the fun.

The days of the month are calculated from the period of the full moon, and the number of them is divided into two equal parts.

To the portion of days comprized in the increafing half of the moon, they give the name of Sood, or filling; and the other, they term Bole, or the Wain.

The

The Jogue is divided into luftra of twelve years, each of which is diftinguifhed by its peculiar denomination.

The obfervatory at Banaris is an undeniable proof of the knowledge which the Hindoos have acquired in the motions of the celeftial bodies.

Could accefs be gotten to fuch records of the Hindoos, as are unaccompanied with that redundancy of fable, with which their priefts have fo copioufly interwoven them, it would not be prefumptuous to fuppofe, that we fhould difcover they were, in the more early age of the world, one of the moft enlightened and powerful nations then inhabiting the face of the earth.

Their empire, as related in many of their hiſtorical tracts, conſiſted of fifty-ſix ſeparate principalities, ultimately governed by one ruler, whoſe kingdom extended from the ſouthern borders of Tartary to the iſland of Ceylon, and from the confines of Aſſam and Arracan to the river Indus.

This immenſe territory was inhabited by a people divided into four diſtinct tribes, each exerciſing different functions and occupations, and all uniting in their various branches to promote a general good.

It abounded in fair and opulent cities, which were decorated with magnificent and lofty temples for the worſhip of the gods, and with ſumptuous manſions, gardens and fountains
for

for the pleasure and accommodation of the people.

Useful and elegant artisans, well skilled in their various trades, in the raising stupendous buildings; in the fabricating gold, silver, and the most delicate cotton cloths, and in the curious workmanship of precious stones and metals, all found ample encouragement in the exercise of their several professions.

It were almost superfluous to say, that if some glaring indulgences in favor of the sacred tribe are excepted, Hindustan must have been governed by salutary and well digested laws.

From the translation of the code by Mr. Halhed, it is seen, that a well chosen system of equitable regulations directed

directed the Hindoos in the punishment of crimes, and for the security of property.

The traveller was enabled to journey through this extensive empire with an ease and safety unknown in other countries.

The public roads were shaded with trees; at every halting place a caravan-sera, with a pond or a well pertaining to it, was founded for the conveniency of the passenger, and should he in any part of the country have been pillaged, and could produce a testimony of his loss, the district in which the damage had been sustained was obliged to make restitution.

When this empire, its polished people, and the progress which art and science

science have made amongst them, are attentively confidered and reflected on; when, at the fame periods, a retrofpective view is thrown on the ftates of the European world, then immerfed in, or only immerging out of ignorance and barbarity, we muft behold Hinduftan with a wonder and refpect; and we may affert, without forfeiting a claim to truth and moderation, that, however far the weftern nations have, in improvements and refinement, outftripped the followers of Brimhah, yet in the more early periods of life, they, certainly did poffefs valuable materials of philofophy and ufeful knowledge.

The humane mind, will, naturally, be impreffed with a fenfe of forrow and pity for a people who have fallen from

from so conspicuous a height of glory and fortune, and who, perhaps, have contributed to polish and exalt the very men who now hold them in subjection.

To form a satisfactory judgment of the genius of the Hindoos, or to describe, with a due accuracy, the degree to which they raised art and science, it were requisite, if the necessary materials could be procured, that we did endeavour to exhibit a view of the situation in which these people were placed before they were conquered by the victorious followers of Mahomed.

A partial and a very degrading relation would be made of them, were the description of their laws, government and manners, taken from the appearance

ance they make in the eye of the world at this day.

The empire of Hinduſtan was overthrown by a fierce race of men, who in their furious courſe of conqueſt, exerted the moſt ſtrenuous efforts, in levelling every monument of worſhip and taſte.

They maſſacred the prieſts and plundered the temples, with a ſpecies of keenneſs and ferocity, which their prophet, himſelf, might have gloried in.

A people thus cruſhed, groaning under the load of oppreſſion, and diſmayed at the ſight of ſuch cruelties, muſt ſoon have loſt the ſpirit of ſcience and the exertion of genius.

Particularly, as their fine arts were fo blended with the fyftem of religion, that the perfecution of the one muft have fhed the moft baneful influence on the exiftence of the other.

To decide on, or affix the character of the Hindoo, from the point of view in which he is now beheld, would be in fome degree tantamount to an attempt of conveying to the mind an exact idea of antient Greece, from the materials now prefented by that wretched country.

The difquifition of the man of philanthropy, and who has fhaken off the fetters of prejudice, will be far different; he will enjoy an heart-felt pleafure in contributing his aid towards difpelling the mortifyng cloud, which

which hath long inveloped the hiſtory of the Hindoo.

This candid inveſtigator will carry him back to that æra of grandeur which his country enjoyed in her day of proſperity, and there hold him out for the infpection and information of mankind; the generality of whom, whether from motives of contempt or habits of indolence, have acquired but a trivial and a very incorrect knowledge of this antient people.

It will then be ſeen, that the genius of the Hindoos was ſo happily led on, and their bent of difpoſition ſo aptly regulated and attempered by the rules eſtabliſhed for the performance of their ſeveral occupations and profeſ- ſions, that we are forcibly induced to enter-

entertain a moft refpectable opinion of the equity of their laws and the wifdom of their government.

A precifion, which eradicated the idea of an error, prefcribed to them their refpective duties in the ftate and in fociety, and wholly precluded any one fect from infringing on the privileges of another.

The Bramin, was invefted with uncontrolable power in all matters of religion; he became the invariable medium, through which the three inferior claffes addreffed their God; he was alfo the fole repofitory and difpenfer of fcience, and to his care and ability was intrufted the education of youth.

The

The importance of thefe offices muft have given to the Bramin great fway in a community, where the attaining at a knowledge of the mode of worfhip from its inexpreffible variety of ceremony, becomes a tafk of arduous labor, and where at the fame time it is deemed an obligation indifpenfably incumbent on the Hindoo for his future welfare, that he be well verfed in the performance of the rites of his religion.

Thefe employments were judged of fufficient magnitude to occupy the ftudy and attention of the Bramin, and he was ftrictly prohibited from engaging in any temporal concern.

The authority of exercifing every function of royalty feems to have devolved, without a referve, on the Chittery

Chittery or Rajah, and his poffeffions were held hereditary in the line of legitimate male primogeniture.

The younger branches of this race had commands in the army beftowed on them, and they were commonly entrufted with the charge of the forts and the ftrong holds of the country.

The occupation of a merchant, with the tranfaction of every fpecies of traffic, was delivered over to the Bhyfe or Baniam, and it was declared unlawful for the other tribes to engage in any branch of commerce.

The hufbandman, the artifan, the common foldier and the labourer, compofed the fooder, or the fourth caft of the Hindoos, and each of thefe refpective respective professions was strongly guarded against encroachments.

Thus distinctly arranged and on the severest penalties, interdicted from any extraneous mixture or the admission of proselytes, the Hindoo government acquired an uniformity and a vigor, the natural result of its happy principles.

Were an analogy ascertained between the mythology of the Hindoos and the Egyptians, very perceptible traces of which present themselves, it may then become a matter of doubt, which people for the greatest space of time have been the most polished and enlightened.

From the adductions which I have brought forward, for the explanation of of some of the most essential tenets of the mythology of the Hindoos, and for the general demonstration of the antiquity of that nation, it may appear to you, that I maintain the doctrine of Egypt's having received a portion of her stock of science and religion from India.

With a deference to popular opinion, but without the prepossessed determination of fabricating a system and adapting to it partial arguments, cautiously selected for its support, I will confess to you, that I am a follower of the belief.

One fact, amongst some others, has afforded me a satisfactory proof of the high antiquity of the Hindoos, as a civilized nation, and marks the

strongest

ſtrongeſt diſapprobation of any foreign intercourſe.

They are forbidden to croſs the river Attoc, the name of which, in many dialects of their language, ſignifies prohibition, and ſhould they paſs this boundary, they are immediately held unclean, and in the ſtrict ſenſe of their religious law, forfeit their rank in the tribes they may be claſſed in.

It is not, therefore, reaſonable to ſuppoſe that any part of a people, under this reſtriction, and who ſeem to have been ſo centred in themſelves, as to poſitively reject the admiſſion of proſelytes, would have emigrated into a diſtant country, and bring from thence a ſyſtem of religious worſhip.

Let

Let me conclude this comparative review with obferving, that—When we fee a people who were poffeffed of an ample ftock of fcience and well digefted rules, for the protection and improvement of fociety, and who profeffed a religious creed, whofe tenets confift of the utmoft refinement and variety of ceremony, and at the. fame time, obferve, amongft other Afiatic nations, and the Egyptians of former times, but partial diftributions of this knowledge, law and religion, we are led to entertain a fuppofition—that the proprietors of the leffer have been fupplied from the fources of the greater fund.

If the pofitions which I have ftated, are thought to convey reafon, they will afford greater pleafure to the man of curious

curious study than those unsubstantial and confused chronological proofs, which are often framed as they may most commodiously accord with some favorite Hypothesis.

Amongst the Hindoos, marriage*, when it can be performed with any degree of conveniency, is deemed a religious duty of an indispensable nature; and it is believed, that propagating species in that state, entitles parents to singular marks of divine favor.

* This word, in the Sumscrit language, signifies pleasure. The Hindoos in common usage have but one wife, and when this rule is deviated from, it is considered as an indecency. There is a set of mendicants, called Joquees or Byraghees, who live in a state of celibacy, but it is not a numerous one.

They shew a disapprobation of celibacy by many marks of opprobrium and scorn; and, I have frequently observed, that when a Hindoo has been asked if he was a married man, he has appeared disconcerted, and ashamed at the fact obliging him to answer in the negative, and immediately attributed the cause of his situation to some particular misfortune.

It is to this institution, which is so strongly recommended, and from a stigma being affixed on the non-obedience to it, I may say, even enforced—that the generally great population of Hindustan, and its speedy recovery after the calamities of war and famine, must be largely ascribed.

The

The entire fyftem of the domeftic ordinances and œconomy of the Hindoos, is founded on a ftrong, yet a fimple bafis, out of which arife effects the moft happy in themfelves, and powerfully operative in uniting the leading bonds of fociety.

From the eftablifhed laws and ufage of the country, the wife depends for the enjoyment of every pleafure, as well as for the mere ordinary accommodations of life, on the immediate exiftence of her hufband.

It becomes her invariable intereft to preferve his health, and her happinefs is abfolutely centred on his living to an old age.

On the demife of the hufband, his wife, literally, devolves into a *caput mortuum,*

mortuum, she cannot marry again, she is deprived of all consequence in the family, and is divested of every mark of ornament and distinction.

There are certain religious ceremonies not lawful for her to perform; and, in some instances, she is held unclean; but, on all occasions, after her husband's death, the widow is classed in the house as a slave, or a menial servant.

Amongst the three first casts of Hindoos, where the idea of honour is more refined, and is oftentimes carried to an extreme, rather than suffer this gradation, by which every female attraction is extinguished, and the women themselves reduced to the lowest degree of mortification, on the pretence

pretence of matrimonial affection, they frequently devote themselves on the funeral pile of their husbands.

In addition to the dread of so degraded a state of humiliation, the widow, on the other side, is told by the Bramins, that in consequence of performing this act of heroism, she will partake of the most exquisite future joys, and that her progeny will become the immediate charge of the deity.

Though the issue of such a resolution must forcibly affect the feelings of humanity, yet as it would appear to originate in a principle, tending to strengthen a salutary domestic policy, it ought not to be hastily condemned as a custom wholly cruel and unjust.

Conformably to the state of domestic subordination, in which Hindoo women are placed, it has been judged expedient to debar them from the use of letters.

The Hindoos invariably hold the language, that female acquired accomplishments are not necessary; whether for the purpose of contributing to a woman's own happiness, or for preserving that decorum of character, and simplicity of manners, which alone can render her useful or amiable in the estimation of her family.

They urge, that a knowledge of literature would have an injurious tendency in drawing a woman from her household cares, and would conduce to give her a disrelish to those offices in which are centered the only satisfaction and amusement that she can with propriety and an observance of rectitude, partake of; and such is the force of custom, that a Hindoo woman would incur a severe reproach were it known, that she could read or write.

The dancing girls, whose occupations are avowedly devoted to the pleasures of the public, are on the contrary educated in most branches of learning, with the utmost care, and are minutely instructed in the knowledge of every attraction and blandishment which can operate in communicating the most refined pleasures.

You

You will be pleafed to obferve, that thefe women are not obliged to fhelter themfelves in private haunts, or are they, on account of their profeffional conduct, marked with any opprobious ftigma.

They compofe a particular clafs of the fociety they may have been originally attached to, and enjoy the declared protection and fanction of government, for which they are affeffed according to their feveral capacities.

No religious ceremonies or feftival of any kind is thought to be performed with the order requifite, unlefs acpanied with dancing girls, and it is ufual for them on a fixed day in the week to attend at the court of the prince or governor of the diftrict,

either

either to make their obeisance, or exhibit some entertainment.

And as a compensation for such services, they are endowed with certain grants of government lands.

An Hindoo family, is implicitly governed by the male senior in it, to whom there is shewn every token of reverence and respect.

A son will not sit in the presence of his father without an express desire, and in his deportment and conversation observes to him the most affectionate behaviour.

In the course of my residence in India, and acquaintance with the Hindoos, I have known but few instances of female incontinence amongst their

K   married

married women, and not one of direct undutifulness to parents.

I cannot avoid obferving, alfo, in this place, that I never heard of a Hindoo free-thinker, and that their moſt illuſtrious characters, and men of the world, fuch as Scindia, Nanah Purnawees* &c. believe the tenets of their doctrine with as much fincerity, and practife the moſt minute cere- mony with as much fcrupulous at- tention as the fimpleſt peafant in their country.

* Eminent Mhahrattah chiefs.

Extract

Extract of a Letter written at Kachmire, April, 1783.

THE religion which prevails in thefe parts*, is that of Brimhah, and as I have already in a fmall fketch endeavoured to throw fome light on that ancient and curious fyftem of worfhip, I will now pafs it over, with an offer of prefenting thofe remarks to you fhould you ever be difpofed to read them.

There does not exift a greater difference in the manners of the inhabitants of thefe mountains, and the people of your quarter, than generally does between high and low landers of the fame nation.

I took

* The mountains at the head of the Punjab.

I took notice of two usages, which seem peculiar to these mountaineers, that of not shaving the beard, and embracing; this ceremony is performed by inclining the head over the left shoulder of the party embraced, and is never used more than one time at a meeting.

The custom of permitting the beard to grow, proceeds, perhaps, from a certain ferocity and roughness immediately incident to their situation, and predominant in the disposition of all mountaineers; which, prompts them in different modes to shew their disdain and contempt of the softer and more luxurious manners of their low country neighbours.

The embracing over the left shoulders only, take its rise, I would conjecture, from the defire of having the right hand at liberty in cafe of danger.

The women have bright olive complexions, are pretty, and moſt delicately ſhaped.

There is a pleafing freedom in their manners, which without having any tendency to immodeſty, or feeming to arife from habits of licentioufnefs, ſtrikes you, as the fimple refult of that unlimited confidence which the Hindoo hufbands in general repofe in their wives.

I have known the women to ſtop in the way, though a pot of water has been on their heads, and converfe unrefervedly

fervedly with paffengers, directing them with great good nature and civility in the right road, or communicating to them any other common information.

Their drefs I think, is agreeable and decent, confifting of a petticoat with a border, commonly of a different colour, and a clofe jacket, which comes half way down the waift, and, from the bottom of the fore part of it, drops a loofe ftomacher, which reaches to the girdle,

Their hair, which is held by them in as high an eftimation as that beautiful ornament can be regarded by our gayeft weftern females, is plaited and interwoven with black filk or cotton ftrings, ſtrings, which falling down the back, almoſt ſweeps the ground.

Over this dreſs, they throw in a moſt becoming and graceful faſhion, a veil, which ſeldom touches, but never wholly conceals the face.

The women of the principal people are kept in Zinanahs, as amongſt the Muſſulmen, and this practice exiſting in a country*, were little danger is to be apprehended from the inſpection of foreign viſitants, affords ſome reaſon of believing, that the concealing certain ranks of women has been a cuſtom eſtabliſhed amongſt the Hindoos, previouſly to the date of any Mahometan government, in Hinduſtan.

It

---

* Mountainous and difficult of acçeſs.

It was once my opinion that the Hindoos, adopting the ufage of their Muffulman conquerors—who deem females in the iffue of war a lawful prize, had fecluded them from public view.

But feeing thefe mountaineers practifing the fame mode, and knowing alfo that the Mhahrattahs, who are an independent people, and confequently free from the apprehenfions, which the conquered Hindoos may entertain, ufe Zinanahs for their women of rank; I am induced to think, that this cuftom did prevail in India before the æra of the Mahometan invafion.

At the fame time, were I to hazard an opinion on fome of the manners of the

the Hindoos from their hiftory; the beft of which, I am to obferve, is ravelled in a maze of obfcurity and fable, I would fay, that the Hindoos in former times, did not confine any claffes of their women.

But as their manners from the great influx of wealth and luxury amongft them became lefs fimple, though they are a people who have undergone fewer changes than any other, that the Princes of the country produced this innovation for the purpofe of impreffing in the minds of their fubjects, an awe and refpect for their families.

In the different relations of the incarnations of Vyftnou, and in the hiftory of their antient Princes, it is feen, that

that at thofe periods, the Hindoo women had an unreftrained admiffion into the affemblies of men, and oftentimes poffeffed great fway in them.

In the hiftory of Ram, who, you know, my dear fir, made a great figure on earth, I have met with a paffage, which may ferve to illuftrate this pofition, and trace alfo to a high fource, a mode of trial hitherto practifed in Europe.

I will premife, with informing you, that Sree Mun Narrain, the Grand Deity of the Hindoos, together with his indivifible affociates, the Mhah Letchimy and the Snake, with the view of correcting certain evils and abufes which at that time had deranged

ranged the terreſtrial ſyſtem, found it expedient to perſonify human beings.

Narrain, acccordingly, took on him the form of Ram, a renowned ſoldier, Letchimy became his wife, under the name of Seetah Devee, and the Snake was transformed into the body of a Letchimun, the brother and conſtant attendant of Ram.

Under this deſignation, theſe perſonages mixed freely in all human ſocieties, nor is there the leaſt mention made in any part of the hiſtory of Seetah's having been reſtricted from an admiſſion to them.

On the contrary, ſhe is repreſented as bearing a part on every occaſion, where it might have been proper for her sex to appear.

A service of a dangerous nature required, that Ram should leave Seetah behind him, and the party being then in a desart, she was consigned to the charge of Letchimun, until Ram might return.

Seetah and her companion remained some time in perfect security and quiet, when a famed magician, led on doubtless by the devil, who is ever on the watch to draw astray the ladies, came that way, saw Seetah, and became deeply enamoured with her.

This subtle man having discovered, perhaps, by his spells and incantations, that the eyes of women are the soonest ensnared, contrived that a bird

of

of a moſt brilliantly beautiful plumage, ſhould fly full in the ſight of Seetah.

This horrid experiment had the deſired and the completeſt effect; for the deluded fair one inſtantly conjured Letchimun, by every thing he could hold dear, by the affection he had for her, by the reſpect he bore to Ram, to procure for her the charming bird.

Letchimun was amazed and much troubled at this entreaty: he endeavored to expoſtulate on the eminent danger of quitting her in ſo perilous a ſituation.

He pointed out to her, in the moſt lively language, the certainty of incurring the ſevereſt diſpleaſure of Ram, for a breach of his orders; and, in
ſhort,

short, he urged every argument which a regard for his own character, or her safety, could suggest.

The dazzling hues of this bird had taken such ample possession of the mind of Seetah, that there did not remain in it one unoccupied space for the reception of Letchimun's advice.

She must possess this object of her wishes, or she should become the most miserable of women; and, on the repeated denial of Letchimun to comply with her desire, blinded by the disappointment of her fondest hopes, and hurried on by a burst of rage, she accused Letchimun of the design of seducing her, and alledged that as the only reason of his dislike of leaving her.

The

This accufation convincing Letchimun of the inefficacy of his arguments, and the neceffity of an acquiefcence, he immediately went in queft of the bird; but, previoufly to his departure, he drew a magic circle around the fpot where Seetah remained; and told her, while fhe continued within that fpace, that no misfortune could betide her.

Letchimun had no fooner gone, than the plotting necromancer, affuming the appearance of an old and a very infirm man, in a languid and a feeble manner approached near the place where Seetah ftood, and through excefs of weaknefs, he feemed obliged to extend himfelf on the ground.

He befought her, in an affecting and a pitiable tone of voice, to adminifter

to

to him a little water to allay his thirst, and to recruit an almost exhausted strength.

The tender hearted, but ill-fated Seetah felt the full force of the prayers of a distressed old man, and with a bosom overflowing with the effusions of humanity and benevolence, unmindful of her own happiness, she stepped beyond the prescribed bound, and fell that instant into the power of her betrayer.

Here the story sets forth, what would but little contribute to my credit to relate, or your amusement to be informed of; it only now concerns me to make mention, that after Ram had recovered Seetah, he ordered, for the removal of every suspicion in his own breast,

breaſt, and for effectually ſhutting the mouth of Slander, that ſhe ſhould undergo the ordeal trial.

Seetah, eager to baniſh the moſt latent doubt from the mind of her Lord, and anxious to exhibit to the world ſo public a teſtimony of her purity, heard the mandate with pleaſure; and, without any ſhew of dread, walked over the burning iron; but the feet of Seetah, ſays the hiſtorian, being ſhod with innocence, the ſcorching heat was to her as a bed of flowers.

Pardon me, my friend, for thus intruding on you this eaſtern tale, which would be altogether a trifling one, did it not tend to indicate, that the Hindoos

Hindoos had a knowledge of the ordeal trial, at, doubtlefs, a very early period, and that in thofe ages it would feem their women of the firſt rank appeared in public.

The fame ufe may be made of this ſtory, as that which is contained in the Arabian Nights entertainment, where amidſt the olio of talifmans, genii and devils, you are enabled to extract juſt reprefentations of the manners and difpofitions of the people,

As I have thus far entered into a fubject, which has often excited my curiofity, I will, with your permiffion, proceed fomewhat farther, and recite to you a circumſtance which may affiſt in corroborating my belief, that the Hindoo women of rank, conformably

to

to ancient ufages, and to fome now exifting, were not wholly fecluded from the fight of men.

When a young woman of the Rajah or the Royal Race, was marriageable, or fuppofed to poffefs an underftanding difcrimination of choice, fhe was conducted into an apartment, where there were many youths of her own fex affembled, and defired to felect the perfon the moft pleafing to her.

She performed the ceremony, of declaring her fentiments, by throwing a wreath of flowers over the neck of the favored young man, who, if the lady fhould have been agreeable to him, was efteemed her future hufband.

This

This rule, I have been informed, is obferved at this day in Tanjore, where I refided fome little time, and received the intelligence from a Mharattah Bramin, who had an employment at the Rajah's court.

The aforegoing opinions, my friend, I have freely given you, and I am to intreat, that you will as freely diffect and analyfe them; taking fuch parts as may appear to you founded on reafon and natural principles, and rejecting fuch as may feem vague or dictated by fancy.

F I N I S.

www.ingramcontent.com/pod-product-compliance
Lightning Source LLC
Chambersburg PA
CBHW020300090426
42735CB00009B/1163